Art Styles

Post-Impressionism

by Julie Murray

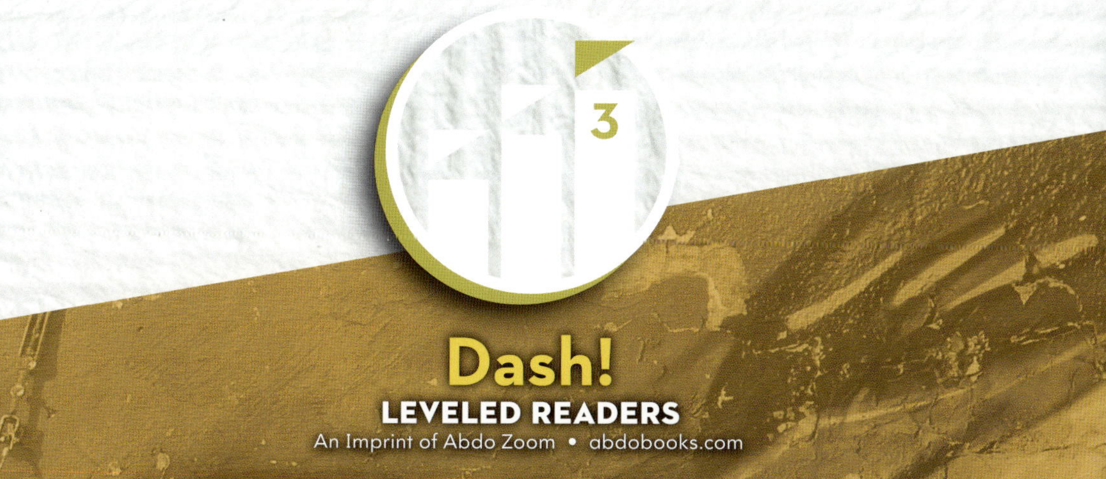

Dash!
LEVELED READERS
An Imprint of Abdo Zoom • abdobooks.com

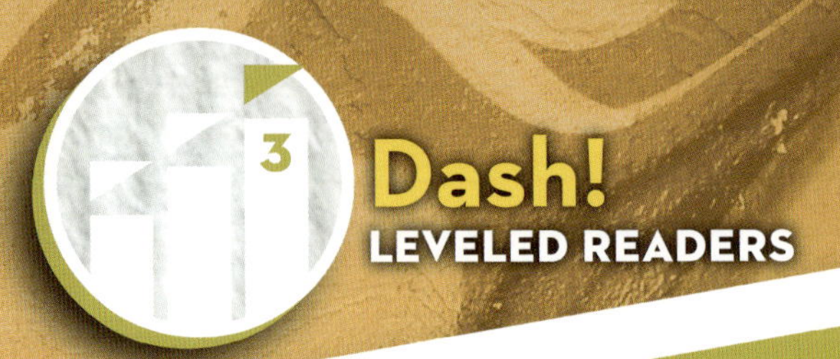

Level 1 – Beginning
Short and simple sentences with familiar words or patterns for children who are beginning to understand how letters and sounds go together.

Level 2 – Emerging
Longer words and sentences with more complex language patterns for readers who are practicing common words and letter sounds.

Level 3 – Transitional
More developed language and vocabulary for readers who are becoming more independent.

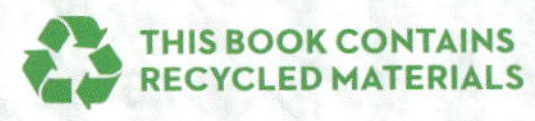

abdobooks.com

Published by Abdo Zoom, a division of ABDO, PO Box 398166, Minneapolis, Minnesota 55439.

Printed in the United States of America, North Mankato, Minnesota.
102023
012024

Photo Credits: Getty Images, Shutterstock
Production Contributors: Kenny Abdo, Jennie Forsberg, Grace Hansen, John Hansen
Design Contributors: Candice Keimig, Neil Klinepier

Library of Congress Control Number: 2023938023

Publisher's Cataloging in Publication Data

Names: Murray, Julie, author.
Title: Post-Impressionism / by Julie Murray
Description: Minneapolis, Minnesota : Abdo Zoom, 2024 | Series: Art styles | Includes online resources and index.
Identifiers: ISBN 9781098283971 (lib. bdg.) | ISBN 9781098284695 (eBook) | ISBN 9781098285050 (Read-to-Me eBook)
Subjects: LCSH: Post-impressionism (Art)--Juvenile literature. | Painting, Modern--19th century--History--Juvenile literature. | Post-impressionism (Art)--France--Juvenile literature. | Painting--Juvenile literature.
Classification: DDC 759.05--dc23

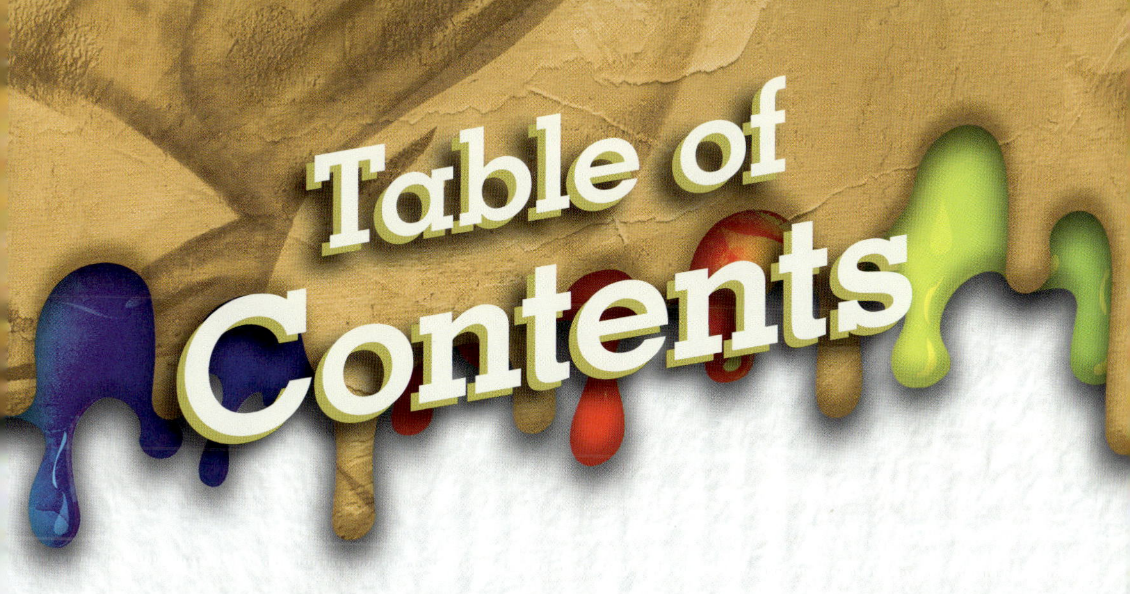
Table of Contents

Post-Impressionism

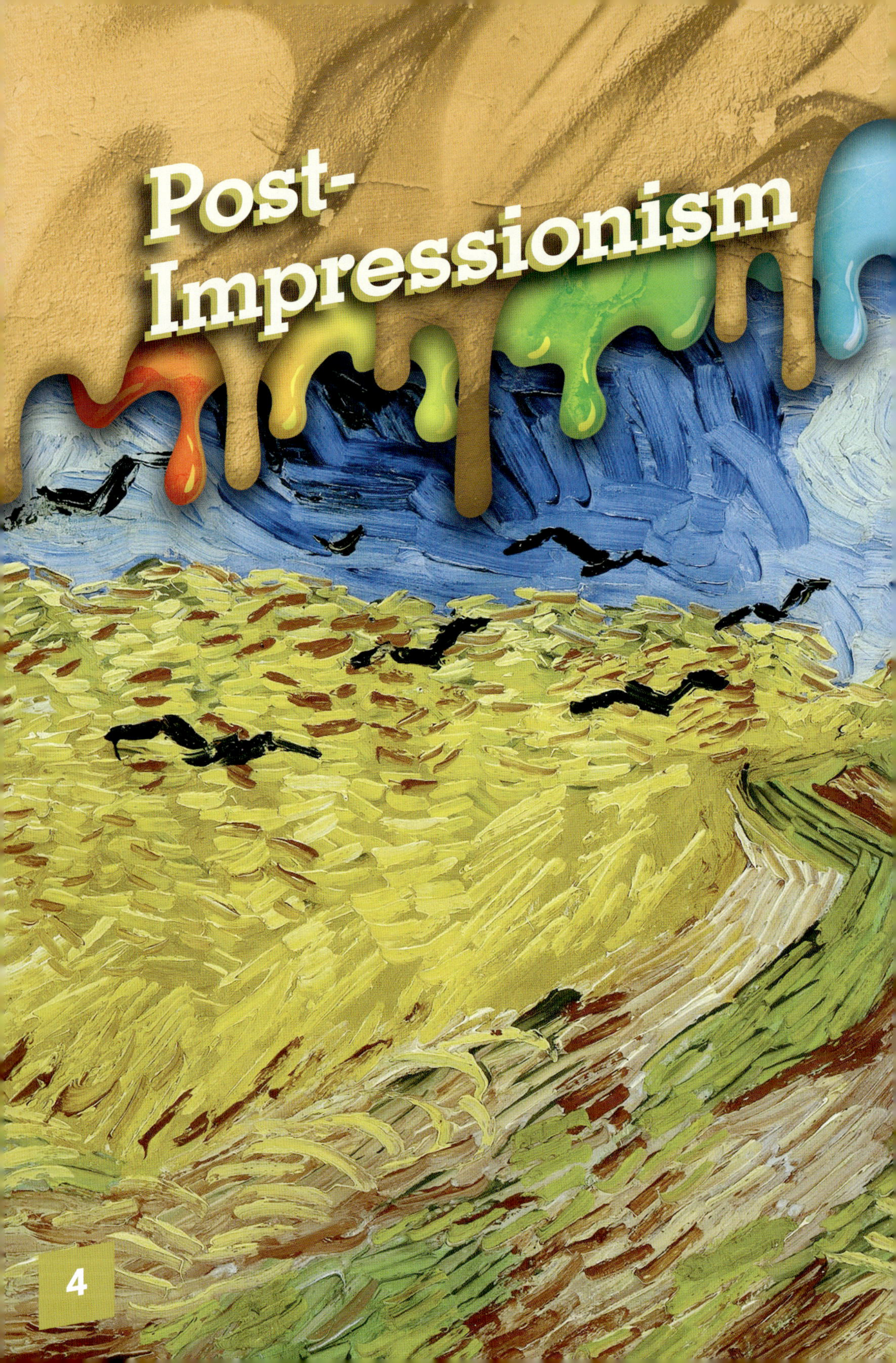

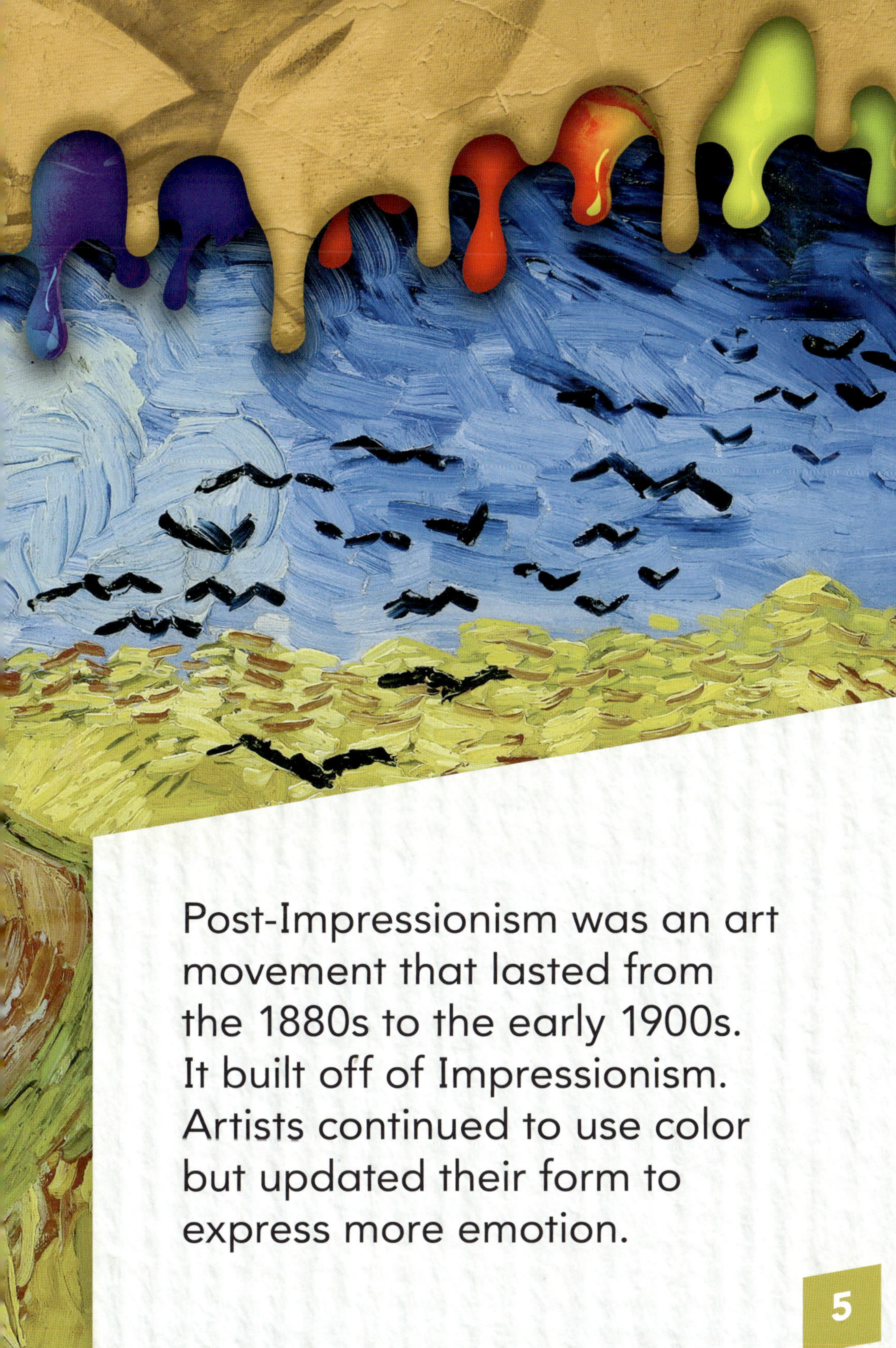

Post-Impressionism was an art movement that lasted from the 1880s to the early 1900s. It built off of Impressionism. Artists continued to use color but updated their form to express more emotion.

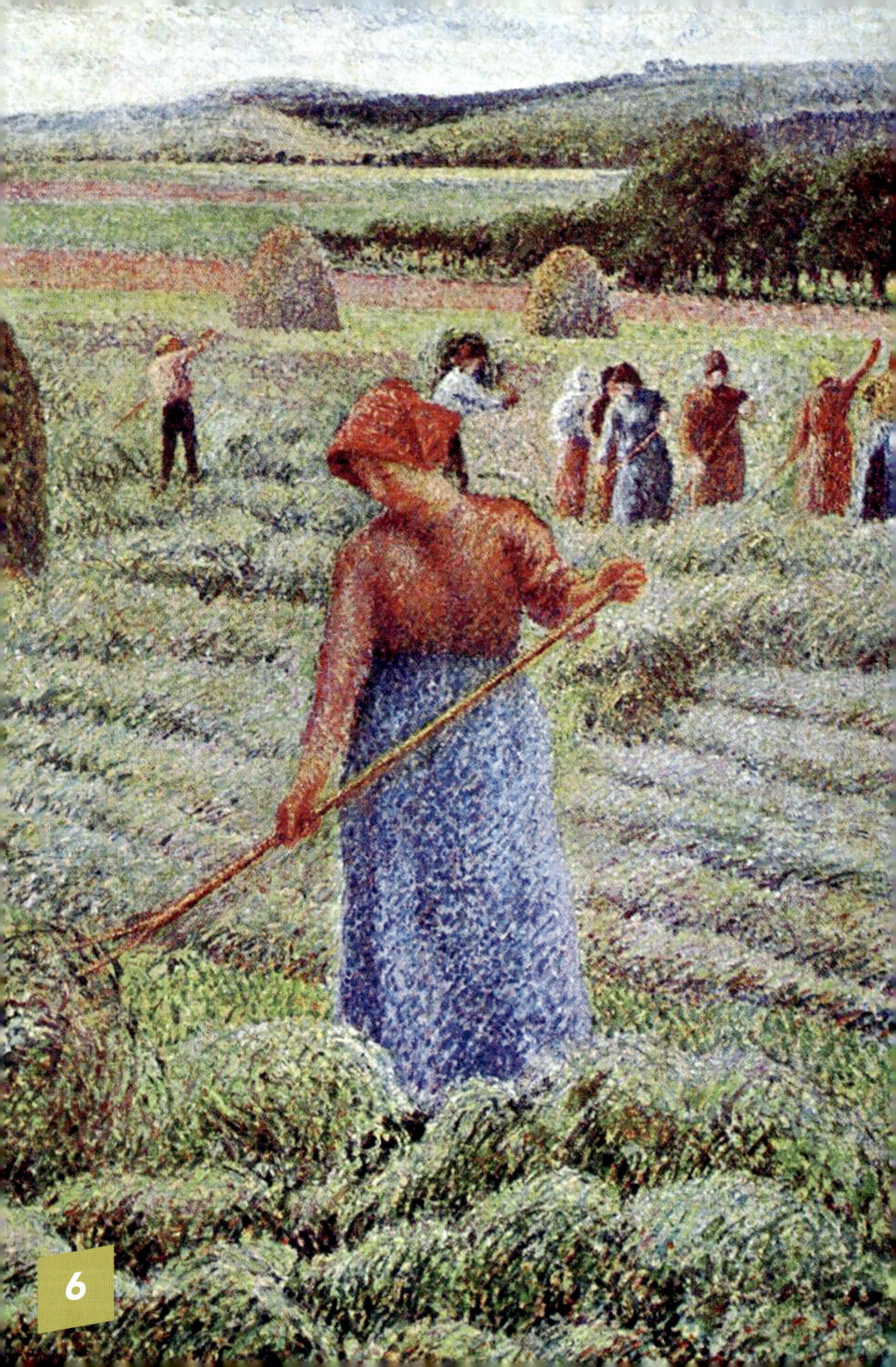
6

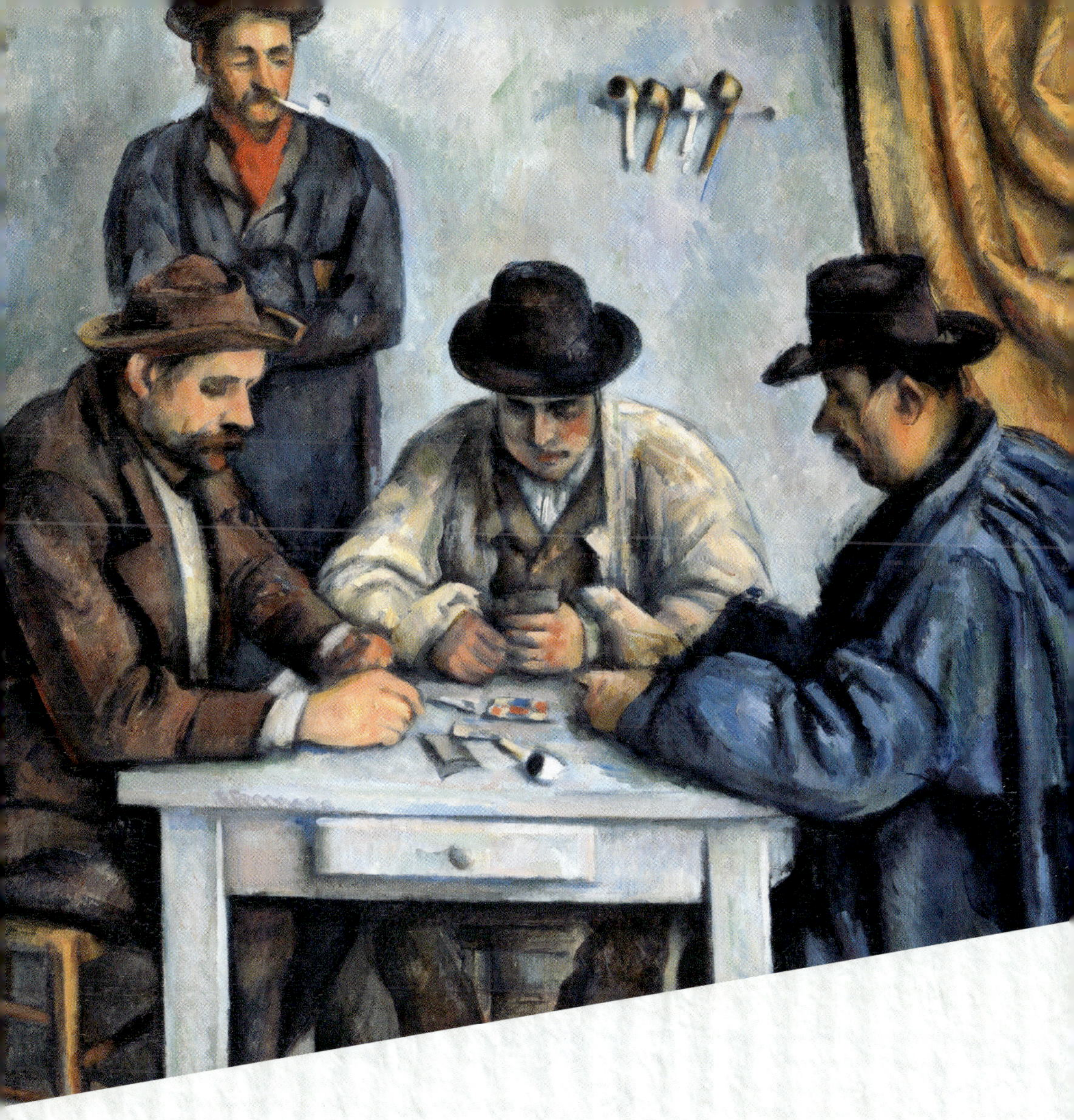

Each Post-Impressionist artist had their own style. The artists concentrated on symbolism. They showed their view of the world in their works.

Characteristics of Post-Impressionism

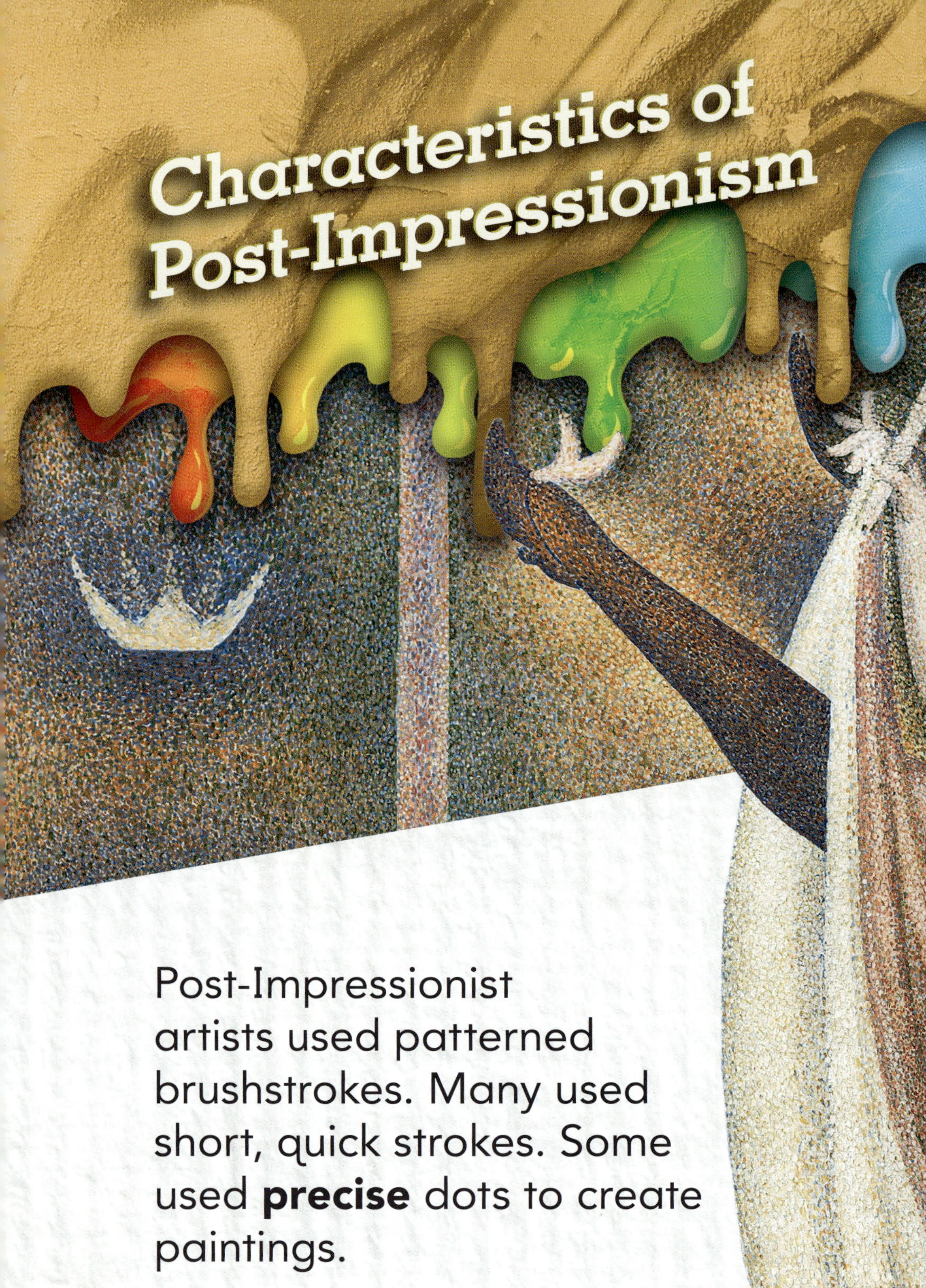

Post-Impressionist artists used patterned brushstrokes. Many used short, quick strokes. Some used **precise** dots to create paintings.

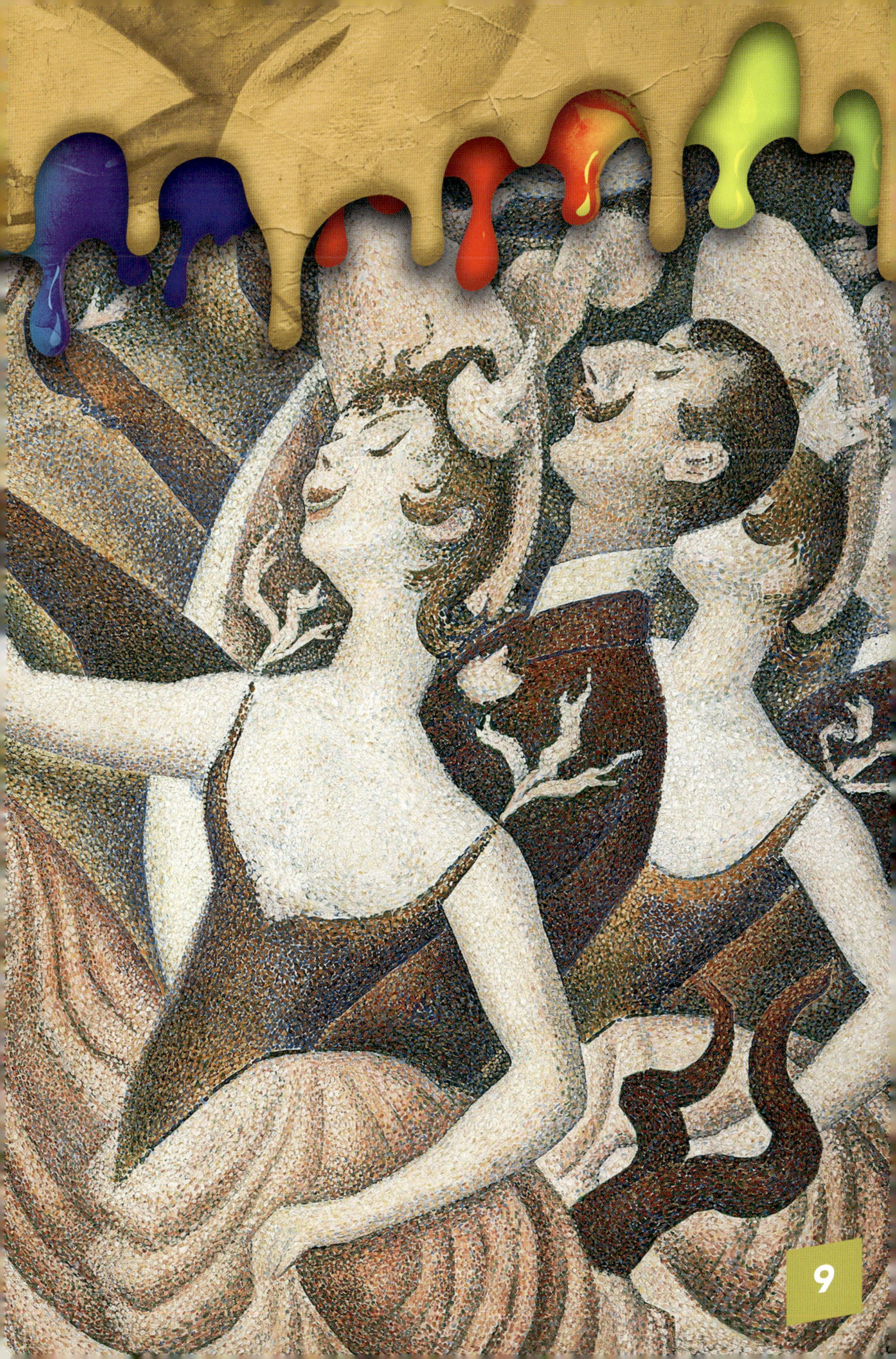

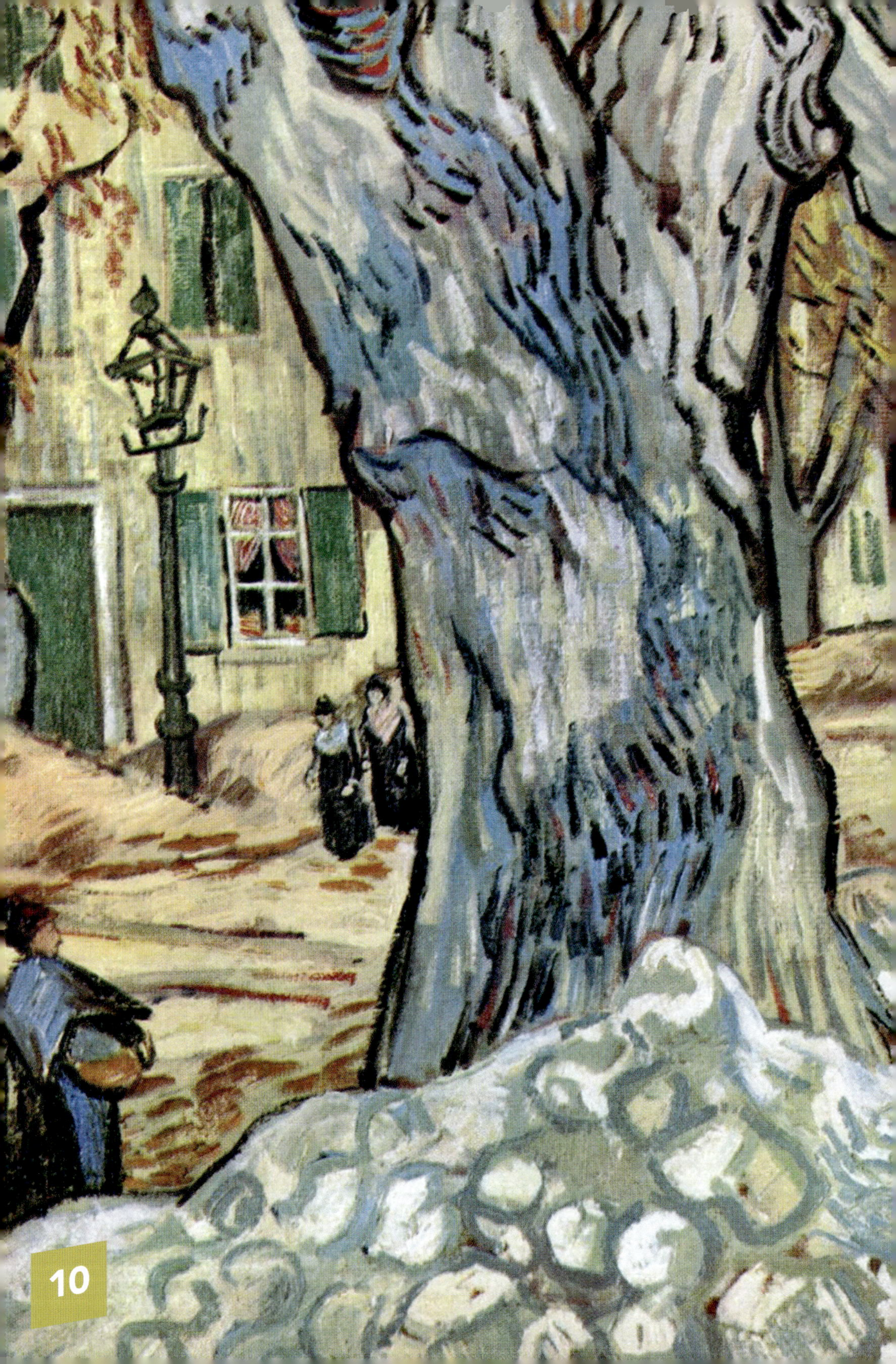

10

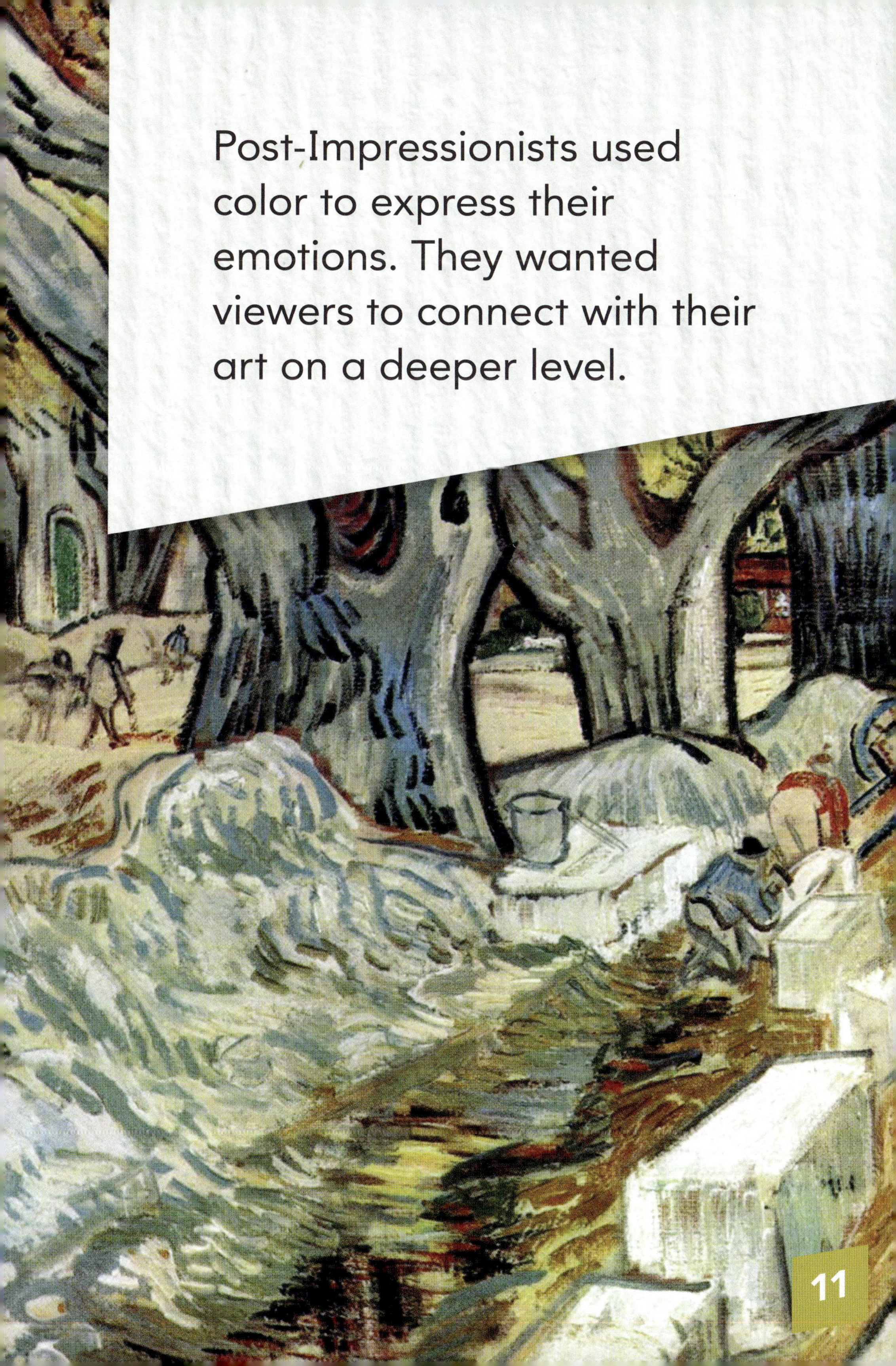

Post-Impressionists used color to express their emotions. They wanted viewers to connect with their art on a deeper level.

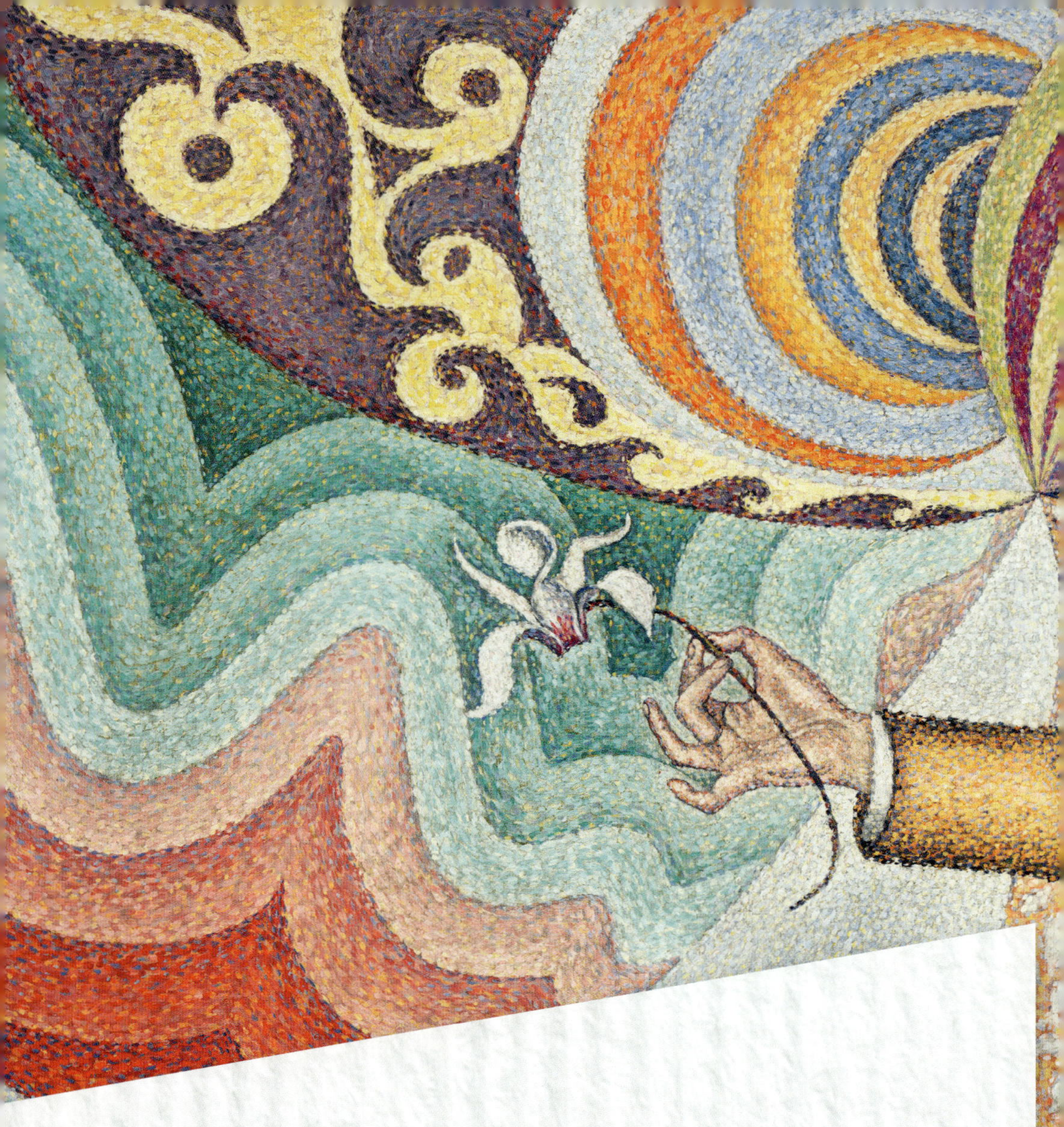

The artists also used symbolism to communicate their thoughts and feelings. Some artists expressed this through geometric shapes and **abstract** forms.

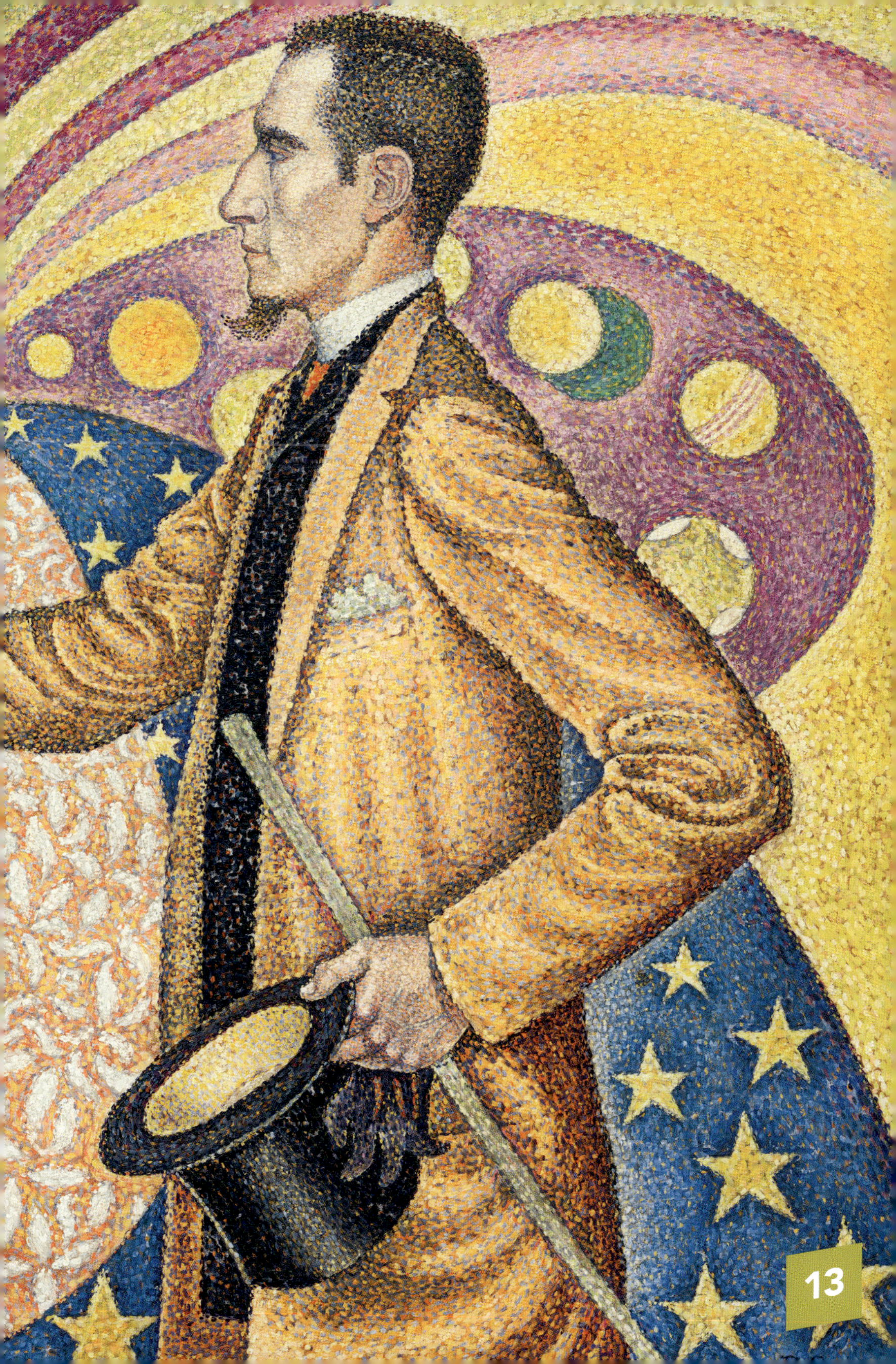

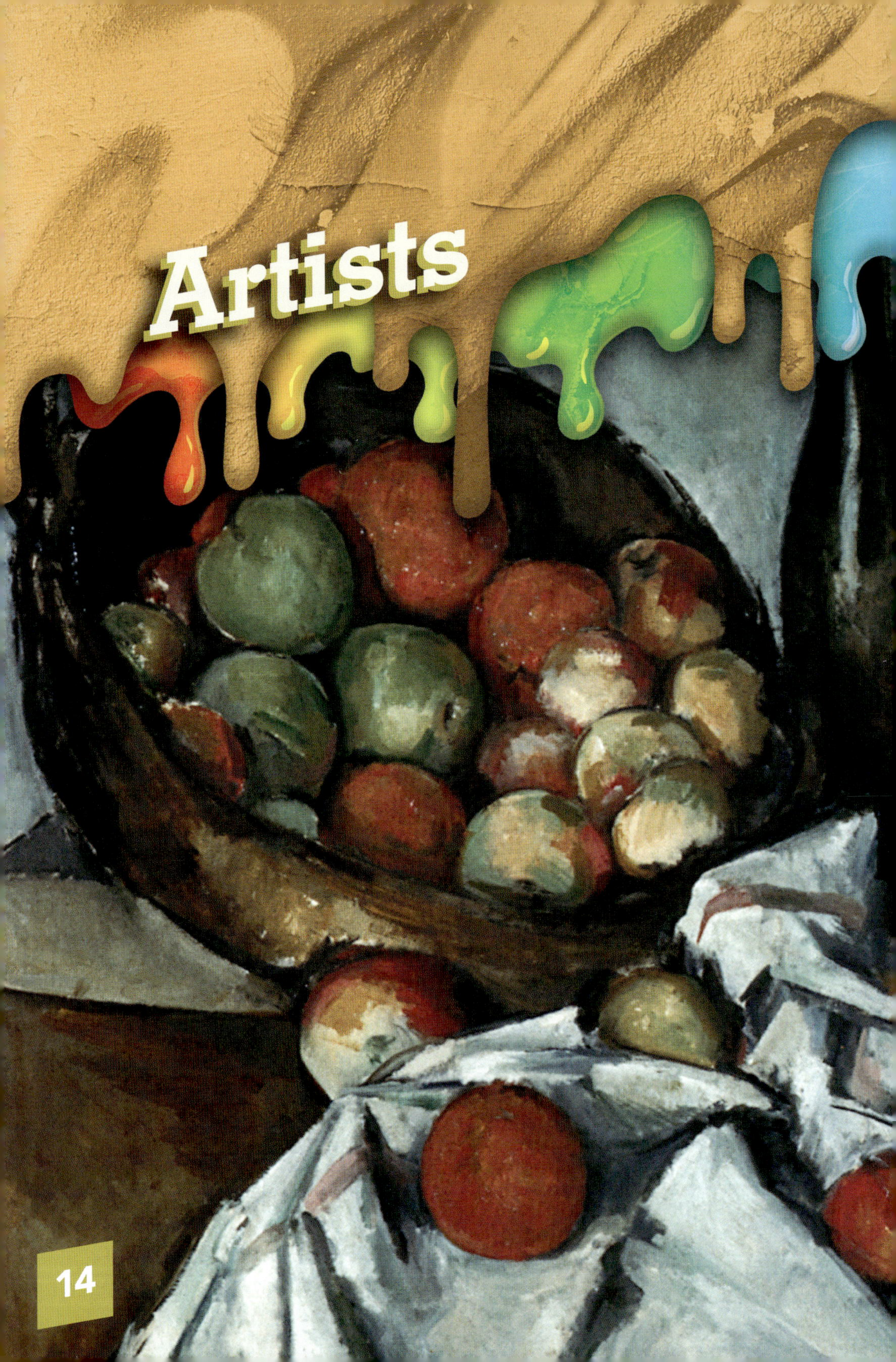

Artists

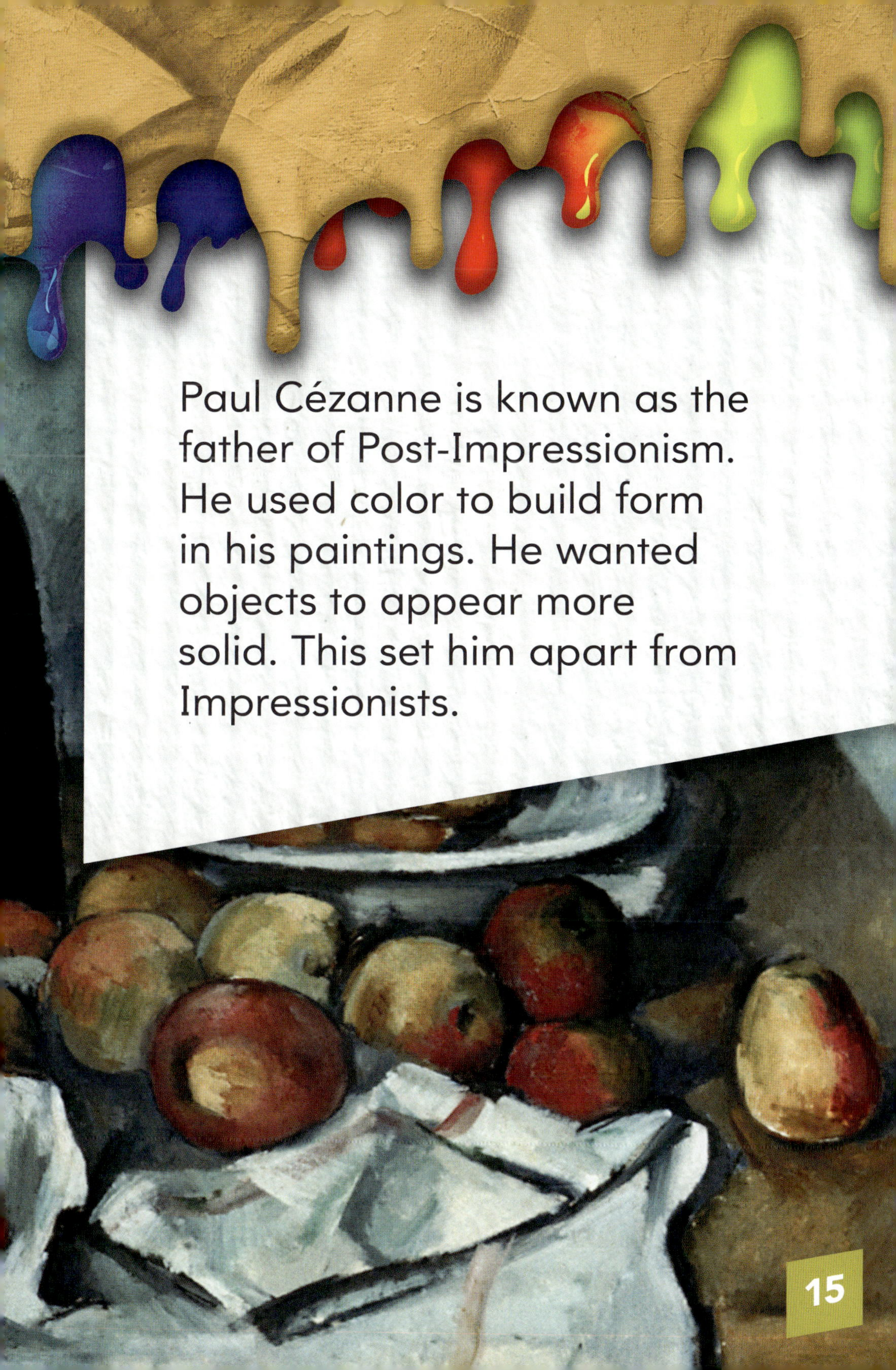

Paul Cézanne is known as the father of Post-Impressionism. He used color to build form in his paintings. He wanted objects to appear more solid. This set him apart from Impressionists.

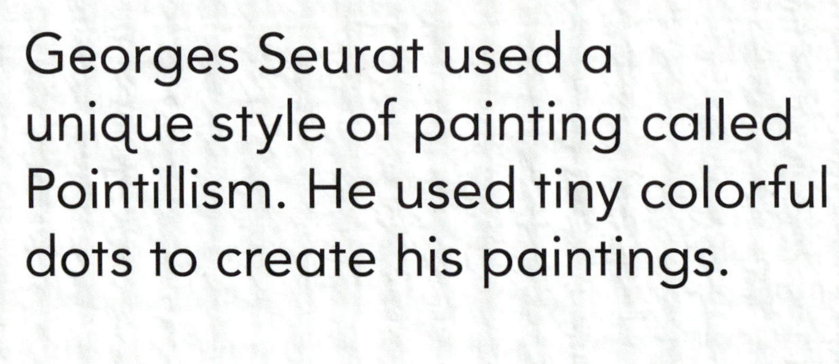

Georges Seurat used a unique style of painting called Pointillism. He used tiny colorful dots to create his paintings.

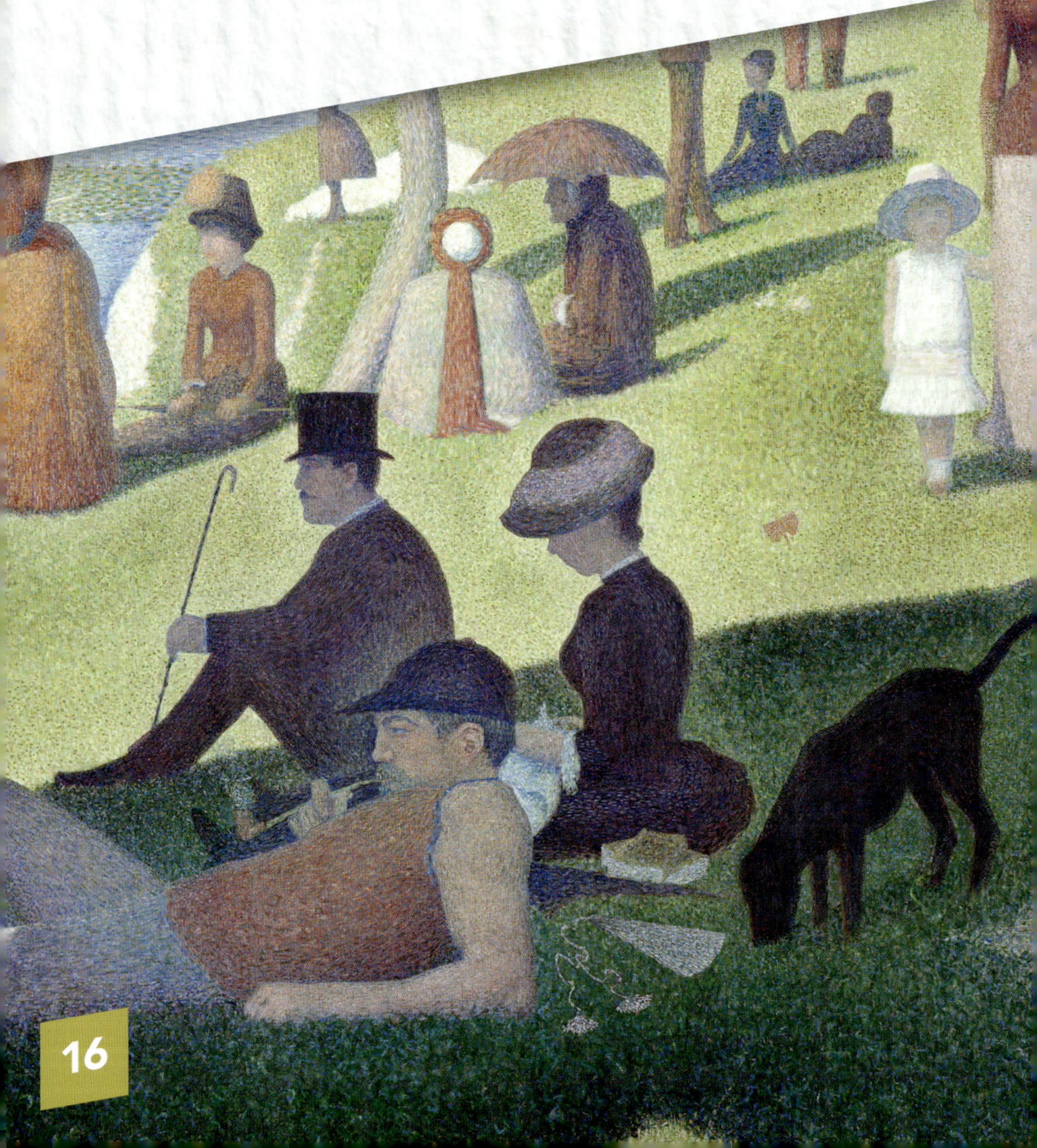

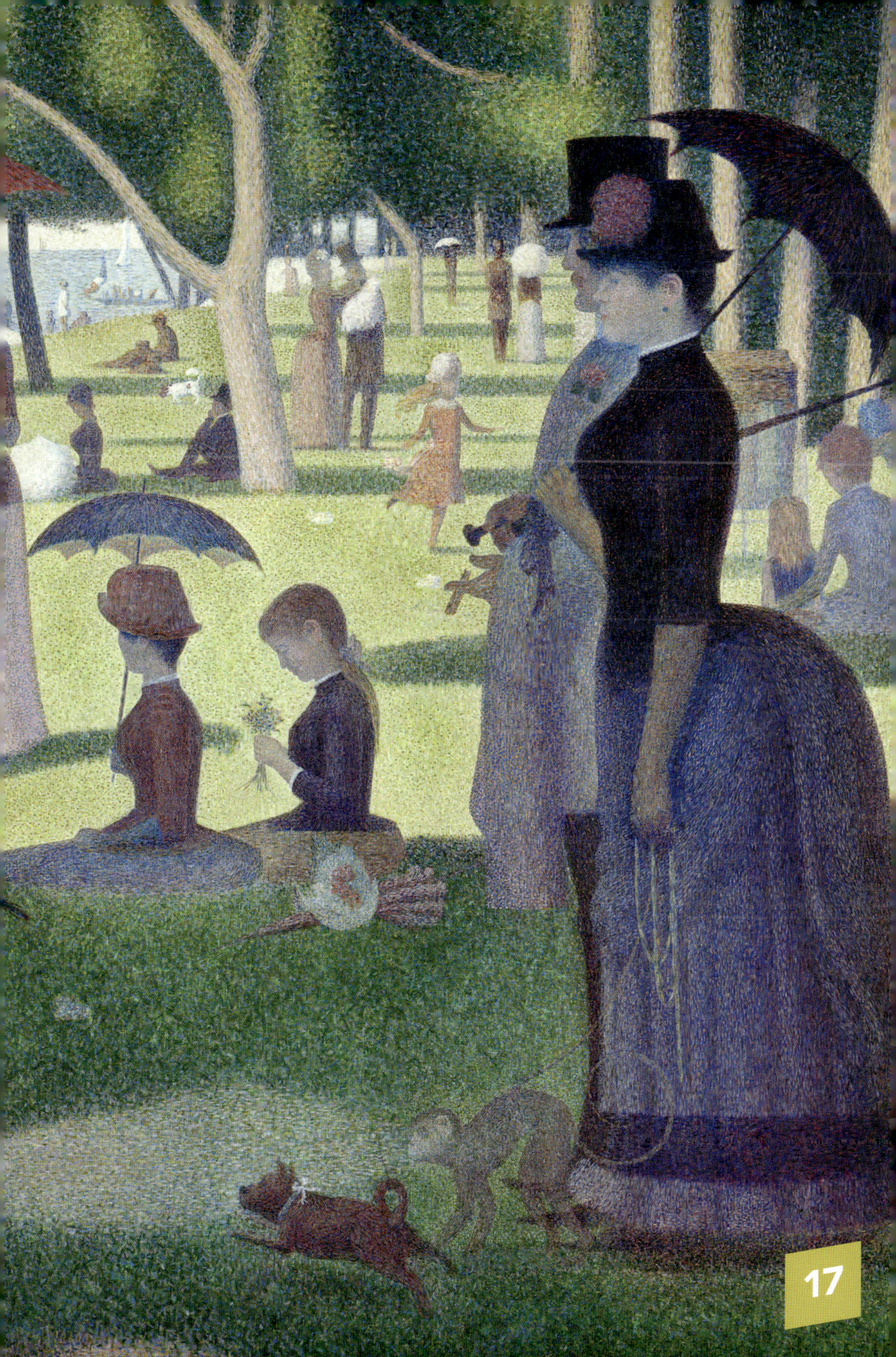

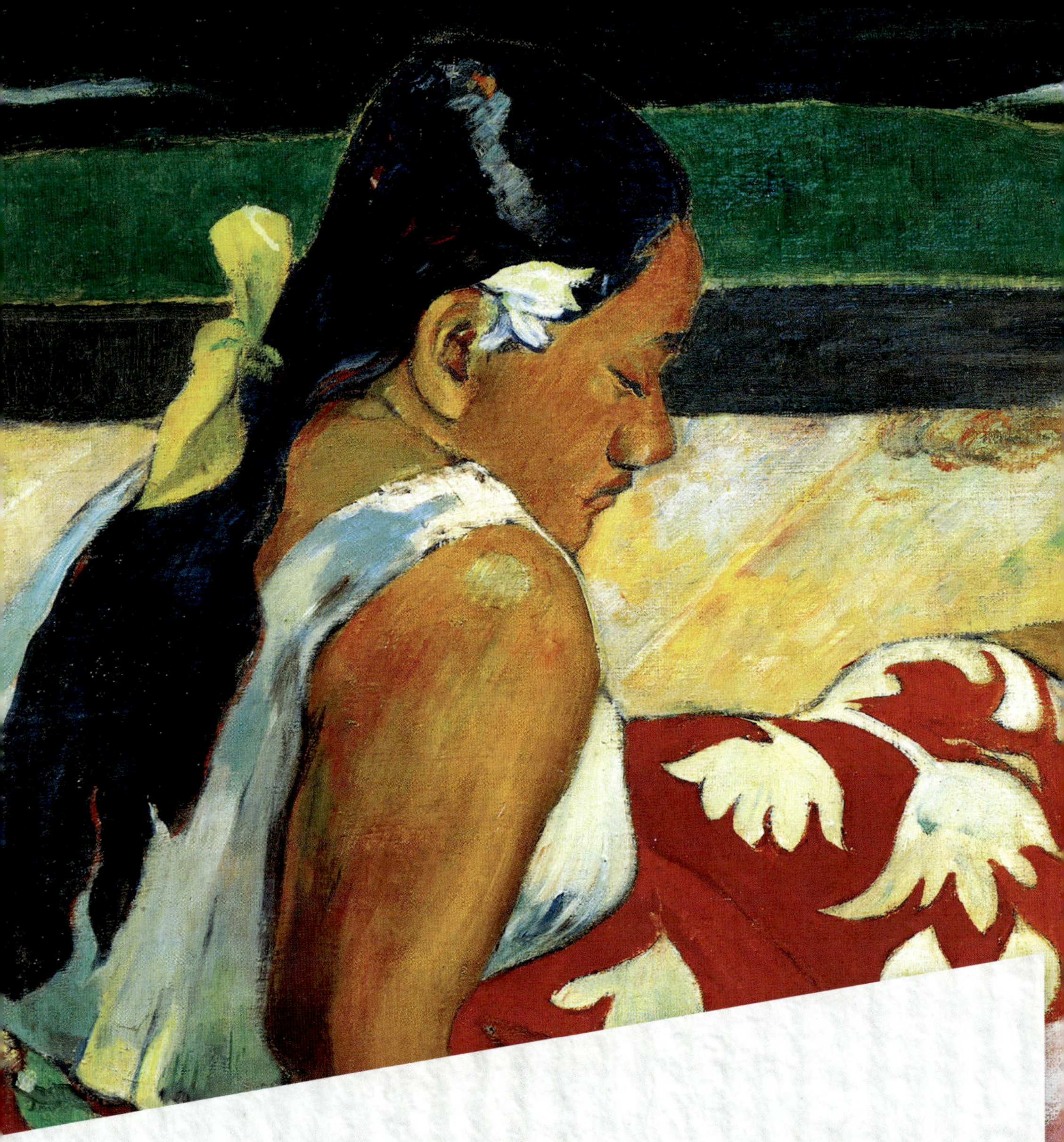

Paul Gauguin lived on the island of Tahiti for many years. There, he painted the people and their clothing using bright colors and flat patterns.

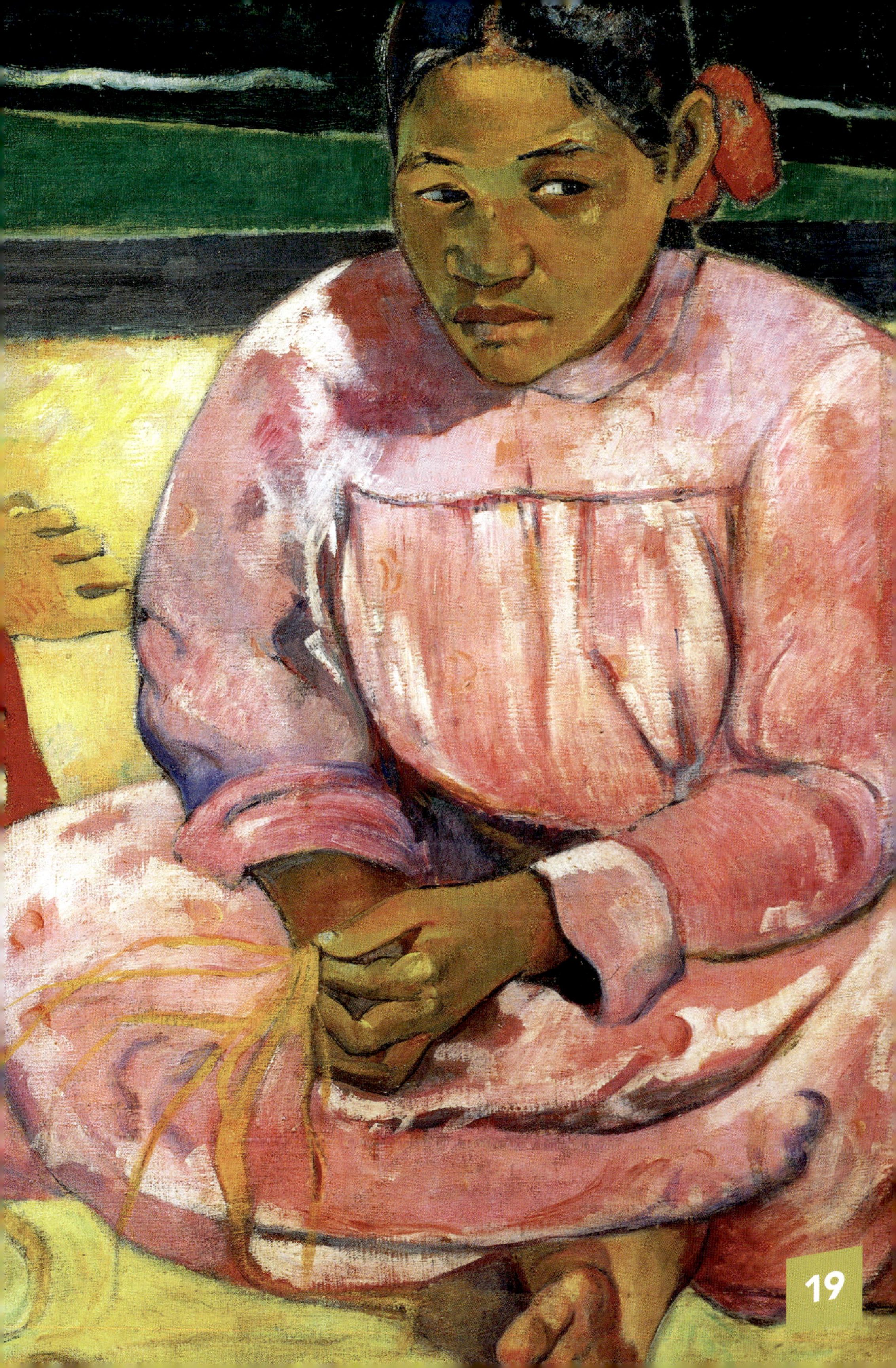

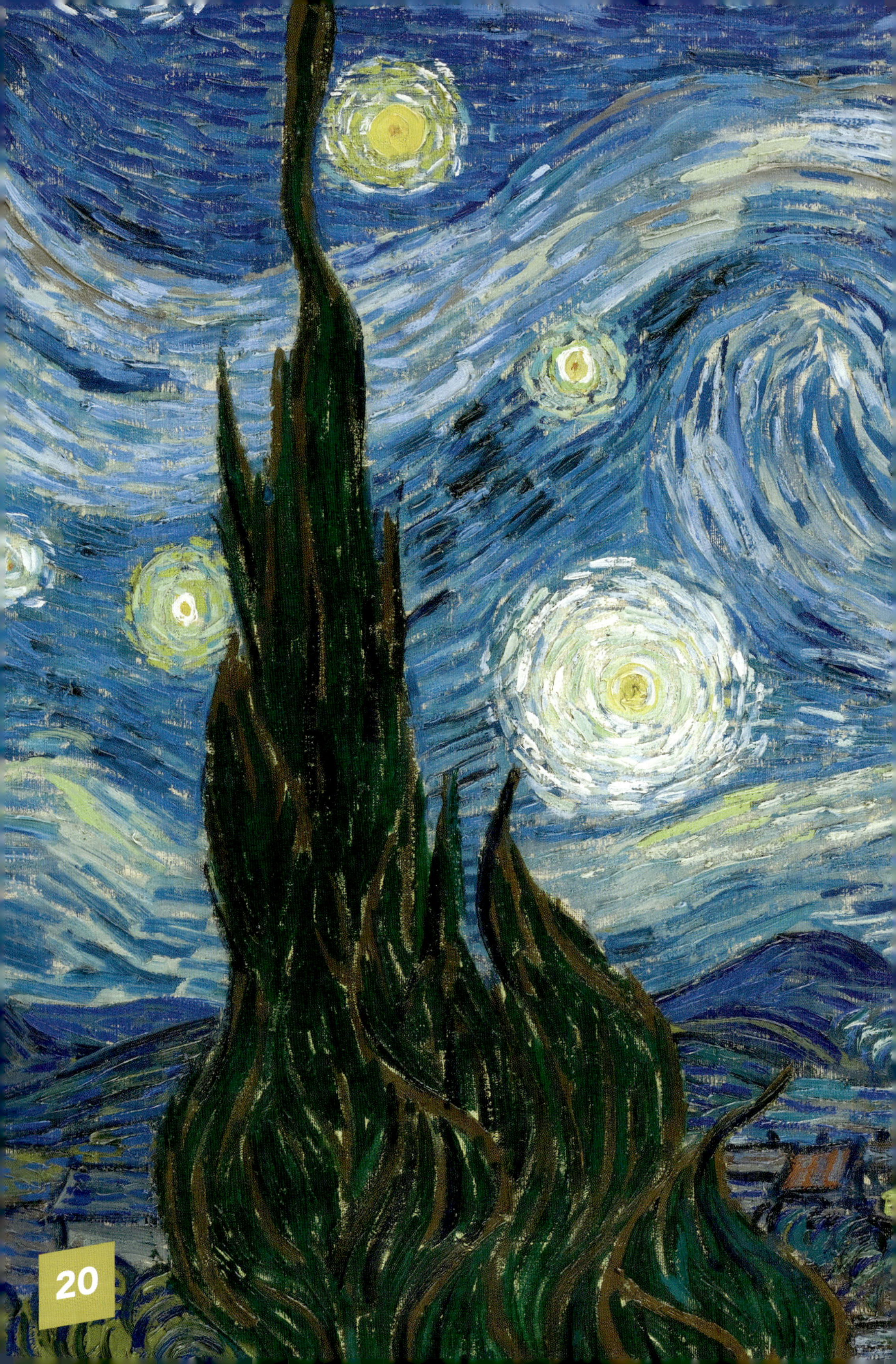

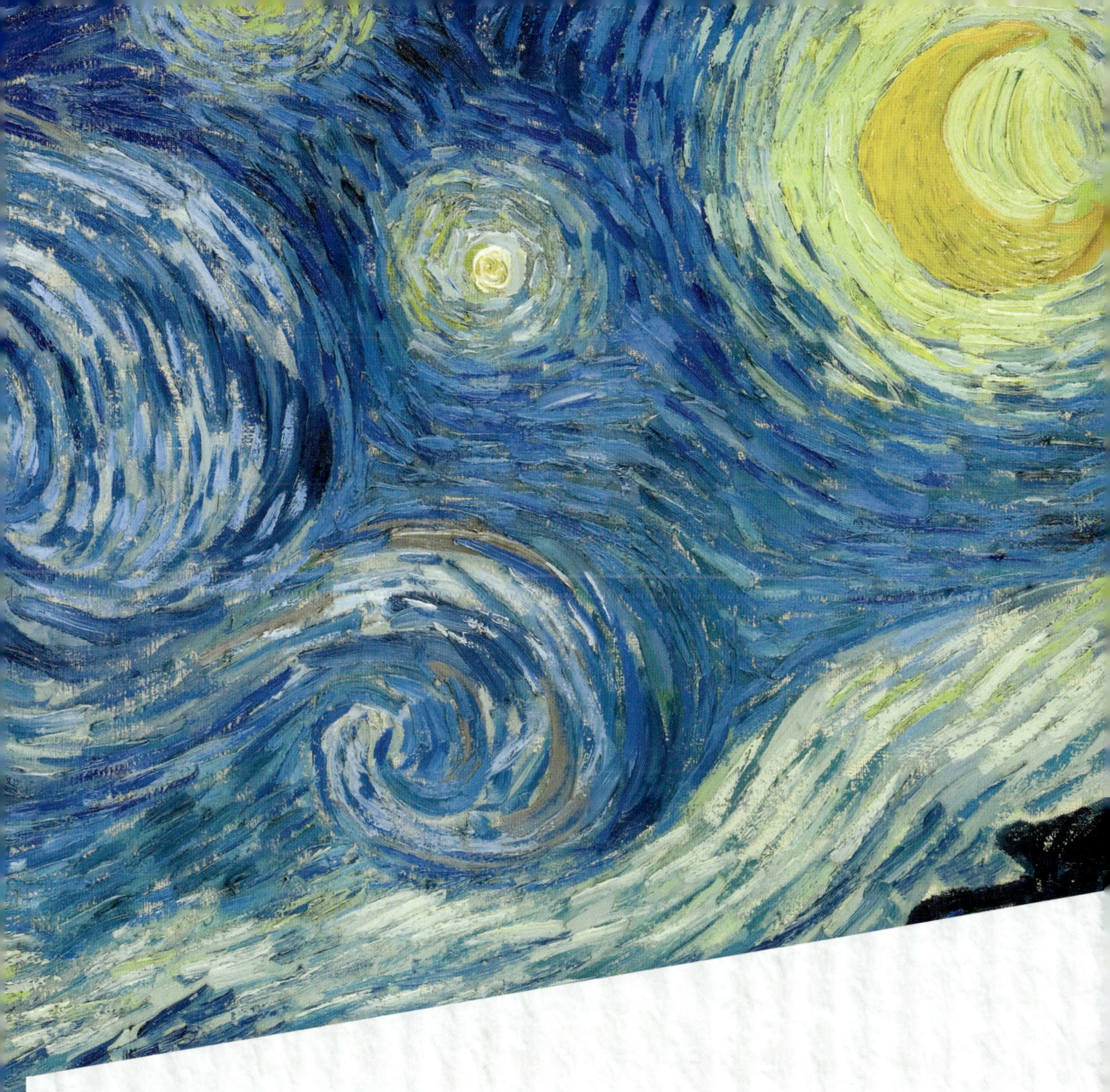

Vincent van Gogh is one of the most famous Post-Impressionist artists. He used bright colors, short brushstrokes, and wavy lines in his works. His emotions came through in his paintings.

More Facts

- The term "Post-Impressionism" was coined by British artist Roger Fry in 1910. He used it to describe the advancement of French art since Édouard Manet.

- Post-Impressionism helped inspire future movements of modern art. **Cubism** and Surrealism are a few of these.

- The Post-Impressionist movement was based in France.

Glossary

abstract – formed in the mind or in thought, with little connection to what actually exists.

Cubism – an early twentieth-century movement in painting and sculpture in which objects were represented abstractly by geometrical forms.

precise – exact.

Index

Online Resources

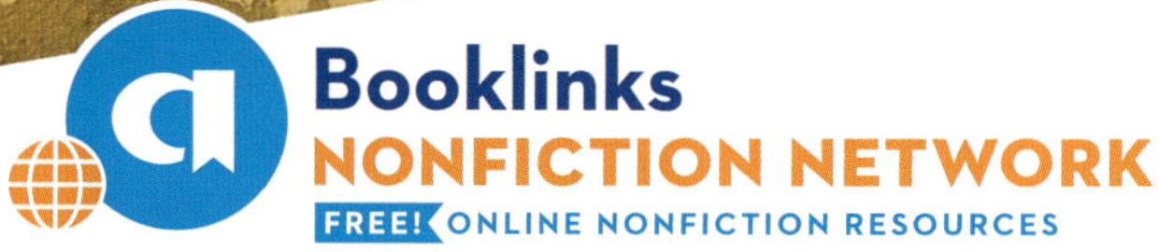

To learn more about Post-Impressionism, please visit **abdobooklinks.com** or scan this QR code. These links are routinely monitored and updated to provide the most current information available.